The Highest Calling

Growing
Into
Womanhood
God's Way

© 2007
Christian Womanhood
8400 Burr Street
Crown Point, Indiana 46307
www.christianwomanhood.org
(219) 365-3202

ISBN: 0-9793892-6-7

CREDITS:
Layout and Design: Linda Stubblefield
Proofreaders: Rena Fish, Jane Grafton, Cindy Schaap

All Scripture references used in this book
are from the King James Bible.

Printed and Bound in the United States

Dedication

I would like to dedicate this book to my mother, Cindy Schaap, without whose influence
I would not have the fulfilled, blessed life I
have today. If it is possible for every
teenage girl to read this book, do the challenge pages, and become just like her, then
this will be the greatest book ever printed.

Mom, you are the epitome of every
chapter written and every word published in
these pages. My hope and prayer is that our
Christian girls will read this and set role models
like you before them and that they would
someday marry a great man, have a happy
home, and rear godly children who will reach the next generation.

Cindy Schaap

Thank you, Mom, for your excellent example and for your years of
love, prayer, and service to God. I still want to be just like you when I
grow up.

Acknowledgments

I would say a special thank you to Mrs. Linda Stubblefield for her many hours of hard work and time she has put into this book as well as hundreds of others. She, as always, did an outstanding job on this project, and I appreciate her so much.

I also would like to thank Priscilla Duff, Stacy Harrell, Jamie Hasse, Joy Jorgensen, Annie Lutz, Trina Reynolds, Ashley Richards, Candace Schaap, Deb Wilson, and Leah Woosley for giving of their hearts and their time in writing the articles for this book. You truly are my friends as well as my heroes, and I admire each of you greatly.

A special thank you to Miss Pam Hibbard and Mrs. Belinda Gaona for allowing me to help with the teen Spectacular—the reason for writing this book.

Thank you so much, Mrs. Jane Grafton, Mrs. Linda Stubblefield, Mrs. Cindy Schaap, and Mrs. Rena Fish for proofing this booklet and doing such a great job.

Table of Contents

Foreword

by Jaclynn Weber

I believe there is a desperate need for godly female role models after whom our teenage girls can pattern their lives. There are too many women in Hollywood, on television, and in magazines who are flaunting their bodies and giving our teenage girls the wrong idea of what femininity and true womanhood is all about.

Todd and Jaclynn Weber

The reason for our putting together this booklet is for you to read and see and learn from some truly godly ladies who have been where you are, have lived through it, and who have made wise choices and are benefitting from their decisions.

I challenge you to read this book with an open mind and heart, to do the challenge pages at the end of the booklet, and to make these ladies role models and patterns for your lives.

CHAPTER ONE

God's Plan for Your Life

by Priscilla Duff

In Romans 12:1-2, Paul speaks about the "...*good, and acceptable, and perfect, will of God.*" Jesus said in the last part of John 5:30, "...*I seek not mine own will, but the will of the Father which hath sent me.*" The Bible makes it very clear that God has a plan for each of our lives. God's plan for my life is different than His plan for your life. I was born in Farmington, Minnesota, to the greatest parents in the world. I was very privileged to have parents who understood the importance of following God's will for their lives. As my parents were on a journey seeking God's perfect will for their lives, I had the privilege to go along on this journey.

Mark and Priscilla Duff
———

My parents moved to Hammond, Indiana, to attend Hyles-Anderson College when I was just four months old. If you can believe it, my parents didn't even ask my opinion about moving. From my earliest years until now, I have had parents in full-time Christian service. My dad served as the principal of Hammond Baptist Junior High School for over 25 years and then was promoted to the academic vice president of Hyles-Anderson College. My mother has worked in the Hammond Baptist Schools for 24 years. I mentioned what a privilege it has been to have parents who followed God's will for their lives, but I haven't always looked at my life as privileged.

As a teenager, I thought I had some rough times being a "Vogel" (my maiden name)—from school teachers asking me, "Do you need to go see your father?" to teachers making me the "example" because "I should know better." Many times as a teenager, I resented my parents' position in the ministry. After all, this was God's will for their lives—NOT MINE! I never asked for the spotlight nor wanted any special treatment. It was a wonderful day in my life when God opened my eyes and spoke to my heart through His Word. I realized that as my parents were pursuing God's perfect will, it was also His will for my life. I realized there were many benefits and also great responsibility in having parents in full-time Christian service.

As my parents served the Lord, I realized that I could either bring honor or shame to the Lord and our family name. When church members speak of your parents, do you bring honor or shame? We need to learn to look to Jesus Who came to do the will of His Father. Christ lived His life for others. Take a few minutes and think of all that your parents have done for you. Stop thinking about yourself and think about how much Jesus loves you. What kind of reputation are you giving your family and your Saviour? Proverbs 22:1a says, *"A good name is rather to be chosen than great riches."* It was a good day when I decided to change my attitude and realize the importance of my having a good name.

It is so important to have the right attitude! I have heard many teenagers say, "I hate that my parents are in full-time Christian service," or "I wish my dad could just work a normal job; life would be so much easier." I used to think that if my dad wasn't in full-time Christian service we would have plenty of money and never have any struggles. God used many godly influences in my life to help me to understand that I needed to change my attitude. I not only changed my attitude, but I realized that I wanted God's will for my life. I wanted my life to reflect what was being preached from the pulpit. I wanted my friends, my pastor, and God to see that teenagers can be happy and joyfully serve the Lord!

I'm not telling you it is easy, but God did give us an example. If you read Matthew 26:42, you will find Jesus praying to His Father saying, *"...O my Father, if this cup may not pass away from me, except I drink it, thy will be done."* Jesus knew He was getting ready to go to the Cross. He would have preferred not to go to the Cross, but He knew the importance of doing the will of His Father.

Happiness is found in knowing and doing God's will for your life.

You find God's will by doing His will. Fall in love with the Word of God, learn how to talk to God, and get busy telling others about Christ. God will show you His will. I have been married now for 13 years to a man who is in full-time Christian service. I also have three children who are on a journey with their parents as they pursue God's will. It is my goal to show them (and you) how happy and wonderful a life can be that is spent doing "His will."

CHAPTER TWO

How to Have a Good Spirit

by Stacy Harrell

Dan and Stacy Harrell

Have you ever met someone who was a real grouch? I mean a real "pickle" of a person? Someone whom you remember as a child, who would cause you to run away crying to your mother if you ever crossed that person's path? No one enjoys spending any amount of time with a person who carries a bad or sour spirit with her! We have all been guilty of conveying the wrong kind of spirit or attitude at some point of time in our lives. With that having been said, we could all use a little "boost" in our spirits now and then!

As we take a look at several areas from which we can learn how to have the right kind of spirit, we need to look first at our perfect example, the Holy Spirit. The Holy Spirit lives inside all of us who have accepted Christ as our Saviour. He, as a member of the Trinity—God the Father, God the Son, and God the Holy Spirit—is available to us constantly as our conscience and Guide. He eagerly awaits to manifest His Spirit through our spirit, throughout our daily lives and dealings with others. In Galatians 5:22-23, the Bible lists the fruit of the spirit. *"But the fruit of the Spirit is love, joy, peace, longsuffering, gentleness, goodness, faith, Meekness, temperance: against such there is no law."* These are some of the foundations that the Holy Spirit offers us if we are yielded to Him. We, through our efforts, are not able to produce this goodness on our own. It is Christ, Who lives in us, Who radiates all the goodness.

Galatians 2:20 says, "*I am crucified with Christ: nevertheless I live; yet not I, **but Christ liveth in me**: and the life which I now live in the flesh I live by the faith of the Son of God, who loved me, and gave himself for me.*"

John 15:5 says, "*I am the vine, ye are the branches: He that abideth in me, and I in him, the same bringeth forth much fruit: **for without me ye can do nothing**.*" We need the Holy Spirit every moment! Dependence upon God may sound like it has little to do with having a good spirit, but depending upon God has everything to do with having a good spirit. If we don't think we need God, then the fruit of the Spirit is unable to be manifested through us. In fact, having a spirit about us that bears those exact characteristics is exactly what most of us want.

Most of us though, perhaps because of our surroundings and circumstances, don't always feel like bearing a good spirit. That is a battle that is no problem for our great God. He tells us in Nehemiah 8:10, that "*...the joy of the LORD is your strength.*" God is able to strengthen us to do anything; all we must have is the joy of the Lord. How fun living a joyful life can be too! It sure beats being miserable!! Let's all make sure that we are asking the Lord often to give us some of His joy and wisdom to be the fruit bearers He intended for all of His children to be.

The Bible says in Matthew 5:14a that we are "*...the light of the world.*" The "*light*" that is being addressed here is describing the Gospel of Jesus Christ. That very Gospel of eternal life in Heaven, through Jesus our Saviour, is exposed to others through **our** lives. As a light that is turned on in a once dark room exposes the contents of that room, we are the light that shines the Gospel upon those that may not know of salvation. Also, as the light in a room comes from a single source of electricity, our light of the Gospel comes only from God. What kind of "light" are others seeing in us? Is our light exposing a godly spirit or a wicked and selfish attitude? Others who cross our paths may or may not become saved because of the kind of "light" that we are exposing. Will we let our spirits "shine" in a good and positive, comely way, or in a negative and proud, unattractive way? The choice is completely up to us.

There are many ways of learning how to gain a good spirit, but if we will first decide to follow our example of the Holy Spirit, and receive the joy of the Lord, then God will give us the strength and wisdom that we need to have the makings for the right kind of spirit.

1. Smile! When we smile, we feel good, and in turn, smiling can make others feel good too. When we smile at someone or someone sees us smile, what might be one of the first thoughts that person might have? Could that individual be thinking, "Oh, she has something green stuck in her teeth!" That very well could be the case, but more than likely, the person will probably just simply think, "Oh, she seems nice!" A smile can do wonders!

I asked my handsome husband if he would give me any suggestions for this chapter, and the advice he gave was, "Every lady and every girl should smile more." Nothing makes any lady or girl prettier than when she smiles. How many of us know of women who perhaps are not extremely attractive, but when we think of them, we picture them as beautiful!

The beauty of a person comes from two areas: from the inside and from the outside. Many times what comes from the inside will overpower what is on the outside, whether negatively or positively. Going back to our scenario of this person about whom we might be thinking, one reason that we think of the person as being beautiful is that the person smiles. A smile costs absolutely nothing. It can be worn anywhere. It takes very little effort. And, in addition to all of these things, we all have one! So in essence, we really have no excuse not to smile! (Unless, of course, we have no lips!!!)

2. Learn to laugh at yourself. There are many avenues of life that are meant to be serious, and rightfully so; but many of us take the lighter, not-so-serious parts of life far too seriously. When we mess up, trip on the sidewalk, fall off of our chair, get caught in a wind storm with every part of us flying in the air on the way to Sunday school, we should just laugh! These are the parts of life that will show or not show our good spirit.

Picture this...a quartet of ladies just finished singing a beautiful special in church. On the way down the stairs, as everyone is giving an applause for a job well done, the last lady suddenly trips on nothing and starts falling head first down the stairs. (Now, this experience [or one like it] is found in all of our lists of fears, isn't it?!!) What should she do, since now she is gracefully sprawled all over the stairs, with her hair covering her face and her limbs pointed in all directions, as the crowd has now stopped clapping and in a unanimous upwards tone has all said, "Aughghghghghghgh!"

Should she:

    A. Start running toward the back door crying hysterically while leaving her shoes behind?

    B. Start yelling at everyone to stop staring while she huffs back to her seat and talks to no one the rest of the service?

    C. Pick up all her belongings, take a slight bow, smile, and walk back to her seat as if it were all planned?

Of course, we know the correct answer. Through much grace and charm we, hopefully, would all have accomplished answer "C" if that had been our story. If we will just laugh at ourselves, we will spare ourselves an awful lot of pain and hurt feelings. Let's not be easily offended, nor take circumstances too seriously. (Besides, we would have been tempted to laugh at that woman too!)

    3. Do not take criticism or compliments too personally. Other's words or actions sometimes hurt us. Whether the hurt is accidental or on purpose, it is just a part of life that we will all be criticized or talked about both from the good and the bad that we do. On the other side, we will more than likely all be complimented on something we've done or said or are wearing. Compliments are always nice, and everyone enjoys receiving them. Dwelling on either one of these, though, is not healthy for a good spirit. If we dwell on the hurts or criticism of others, then our spirit will become bitter, angry, and spiteful; if on the other hand, we dwell on the praise that has come our way, we can become proud, arrogant, and selfish. I heard it once wisely said, "Take compliments and criticism the same way: take it then forget it!!"

    4. Stay away from constant negativity. Whether the source of negativity is from a friend or even a news program, dwelling upon it is not healthy for a good spirit. If we listen to negativism all the time, then that is what will come out through us in our words and actions. If someone close to you is prone to negativism (for example, the glass is always half empty instead of half full), then always be kind, but change the topic or whatever is being discussed to something positive.

    5. Think on positive and joyful things. Philippians 4:8 says, "*Finally, brethren, whatsoever things are true, whatsoever things are honest,* *whatsoever things are just, whatsoever things are pure, whatsoever things are lovely, whatsoever things are of good report; if there be any virtue, and if there be any praise, think on these things."* We need to think on these things also in our music, books, television, and phone conversations. Everywhere we are, we ought to be thinking in a positive way. In Philippians 4: 4-7 the Bible tells us among many things to *"Rejoice in the Lord alway..."* and to not live in a state of worry. We all must think positively and on good, right, and godly things to have a good spirit; not on worry, pain, the ozone, and drug control. Those things all have their proper place, and yes, should be dealt with, but we do not need to dwell on them. It is practically impossible to have a good spirit while we are in a negative state of mind. "Think on these [the good] things!"

6. **Keep and guard others' spirits.** A way we can help watch out for others' spirits is by guarding our own. It is near impossible to change someone's ways, but we can be a good influence on them. If we want our friends to have good spirits, then we first must have a good spirit toward and around them. We must have the joy of the Lord, a positive mind, and a humble heart.

Proverbs 27:17 says, *"Iron sharpeneth iron; so a man sharpeneth the countenance of his friend."* Also, in verse 19 of the same chapter it says, *"As in water face answereth to face, so the heart of man to man."* If we are positive people seeking for positive friends, we'll mostly have positive friends. If we are negative people seeking for friends, then we will mostly have negative friends. Opposites don't attract here. What kind of person we are spirit-wise is what kind of friends we will have, whether we find them or they find us. This is yet another reason why whom we choose as our friends, and yes it is a choice, is so important. We can give a good spirit to others through good words. The kind things we say to or about others will affect their spirit. Proverbs 16:24 says, *"Pleasant words are as an honeycomb, sweet to the soul, and health to the bones."* Proverbs 17:22 says, *"A merry heart doeth good like a medicine: but a broken spirit drieth the bones."* As we strive to have a good spirit, we are not only helping ourselves live a better life, but we are also helping others by using our spirit.

7. **Be faithful in prayer and Bible reading.** When we talk to God, we tend to be more serious, which is perfectly fine, but our Father is a

God of joy! The more time we will spend with God through prayer and talking with Him, we will find that our spirits will be ten times happier and more full of joy than before. He is so good to us. Although the difficult times come to all of us, if we will think hard enough, we will still find many, many things for which to thank and praise the Lord. The Bible says that He *"...loadeth us with benefits."* God is love, joy, peace, and all the good things that we can imagine. He loves us more than we can fathom. We need to encourage ourselves in the good things of the Lord. In I Samuel 30:6b, the Bible says, *"...but David encouraged himself in the LORD his God."* The beginning of this verse talks about how the people were contemplating stoning David because they were mourning the loss of some of their children; yet David, in the midst of that, sought after God and encouraged himself in the Lord.

God is not a genie or a lucky coin; He is Almighty God Who wants our attention, our praise, and our affection all of the time. He sure does deserve it and so much more! Through Christ and His precious Words of Life, we are to live daily depending upon and encouraging ourselves in the Lord. As an illustration of encouraging ourselves, think of one of those "punching bag people." Usually they are pictured as clowns. They have sand on the bottom, and when they are pushed over, they pop right back up. We need to live flexible lives like they do!

When we are hurt or criticized or a family crisis arises and we are, figuratively speaking, "blown down" or "knocked over," we need to have a relationship with God so that we can give everything to Him. If we will do this, then when we get "pushed down," we can come right back up and respond with a good and positive spirit. Often we need to forgive and forget the things that hurt us.

We could also compare our spirits to rubber bands. Mrs. JoJo Moffitt taught us in her college classes to be like rubber bands. We must allow ourselves to be stretched and stretched; yet, when all is said and done, we will come right back to where we belong. Let this be true of us and our spirits.

Many blessings can come as a result of having a good spirit. Proverbs 15:15 says, *"All the days of the afflicted are evil: but he that is of a merry heart hath a continual feast."* Surely none of us want to live out the first line of this verse as evil people (those who hurt others in their sin);

rather, we want to be like the merry-hearted person who has a good spirit and, as the Bible says, "*...hath a continual feast.*" When thinking of a feast, we would probably picture a "mile long" table filled with the most beautiful and scrumptious-looking and tasty food imaginable. To think of enjoying ourselves at that feast continually for a long, long time (if you wouldn't get sick) sounds great! That's how God describes a merry heart. It is such an enjoyable, lifelong journey that is fed by the goodness of our Lord. A good and godly spirit is available for anyone who would like to possess one. It is available from God for all of us. Let us all have a good spirit and a merry heart! Having a joyful life is definitely worth the living!

CHAPTER THREE

How to Deal With Rejection

by Jamie Hasse

My family moved to Hammond, Indiana, from Pound, Wisconsin, when I was going into the seventh grade. We moved just in time to start school and even lived in a hotel for the first week. I'm sure you can imagine how hard it was to "fit in" quickly, especially as it was my first year in junior high. I came from a small school with about 12 kids in my class to a school with 120 kids just in the junior high. I did make some good friends, one of whom is still a good friend to me today (our sons are in the same grade), and I can honestly say that we had a great time. (I have the pictures to prove it.)

Brian and Jamie Hasse

However, I still wanted to "fit in" even more and saw cheerleading as my way to do it. I tried out at the end of my seventh grade year and was ecstatic when I found out I had made the squad. Cheerleading took me in a completely different direction as far as friends and schedule. We had many practices during the summer and throughout the year, as well as games twice a week. It truly felt like I had found my place in school. I loved cheerleading! I loved the fun we had, the friends and memories I made, and even the hard work that went into it. I made the cheerleading squad for my ninth, tenth, and eleventh grade years as well.

I was so excited to try out for my senior year! It was the chance I had been waiting for. I was the only girl to try out who had been a cheerleader before. So, you know what that meant, right? I was basically the captain already! I had never been the captain before but thought I would enjoy it. To be the first girl to start the cheers and to initiate contact with other squads when they visited seemed right up my alley. I remember the try-outs like it was yesterday—can you believe it? After 14 years?!

I thought everything went fine—the jumps, the crowd cheer, the floor cheer, and the one we had to make up. The only area about which I had no clue was the teacher evaluations on character. The judges smiled at me, and one of them gave me a "thumbs-up" when I finished. I think I walked on a cloud for a few days. Then came the meeting where the principal posted the list of which girls had made which squad [junior varsity or varsity].

I distinctly remember his saying, "Now, some of you girls need to remember that cheerleading is not your life, and you may be surprised at who did or did not make the squad."

That's all I remember because my stomach sank. "Was he talking to me?" I wondered. "He's never said ANYTHING like that in one of these meetings before!"

After he posted the list, he walked out and left us to look. Well, I walked up to the board and scanned the list quickly and just thought, "I can't believe it. I'm not on there!" And to make it worse for me, the whole varsity squad was made up completely of new girls.

Now, to be perfectly honest, I laughed (only a little because I was so sick) and thought they were going to become the laughingstock of the school. After I walked out of the room, many people came up to me and asked, "So, are you the captain?" and I actually had to tell them that I wasn't chosen.

Because school was dismissed for the day, I left as fast as I could. On the way home, my mom and my sister asked about the cheerleading squad. I know I was upset, but I was also calm at the same time as there was nothing I could do about it. I think I became more upset later (even years later!) when I was given a reason for not making the squad. I was simply told, "Well, the teachers just didn't like you."

I had a hard time starting my senior year feeling that some of the teachers didn't like me. I was a good student. I think I was fairly friend-ly and got along with others. I felt rejected. Why didn't they like me?

I think everyone asks that question at some point in her life. It was a great time for me to look at myself to see if I was the problem. It became a turning point in my life. I had to decide for myself how I was going to let the rejection I felt affect me. Maybe in the teachers' evaluations of me, they were seeing my potential and doing what they thought would best teach me. Did I want to learn from this or let it ruin my senior year? I chose to move on simply because I had more important things on my mind and not because I was a spiritual giant. I was trying to take a couple of classes at Hyles-Anderson College (of course, which were being offered on Sunday and Wednesday evenings at our church, to earn credits so that I could get married sooner. I also wanted to have the best year ever with my friends. I made so many memories that year that I can honestly say (finally) that I'm glad I wasn't a cheerleader that year. (I will be completely honest with you, though. I remember having the thought that maybe the bus the cheerleaders were on would get in an accident and God just didn't want me on it. Wasn't that terrible of me?)

I also wondered what I could fix about me that people didn't like. Was it the way I talked or the friends with whom I hung around? Did I not study enough to suit the teachers? Should I cut my hair differently? Wear different clothes? I know that it doesn't really matter what other people think about me as long as I am pleasing to God. I don't have to be like anyone else. I just need to be what God wants me to be. *"But godliness with contentment is great gain."* (I Timothy 6:6) Doesn't it feel good, though, to have the approval of someone—especially someone we love and admire? I don't think that wanting acceptance ever goes away. It's just in us to like feeling accepted and to want someone else's approval. We just have to make sure that we are getting the acceptance from people that lead us closer to God.

Sometimes well-meaning, good people can make a mistake and reject you by their actions or by a passing comment. A girl was at a church function some years ago with her new baby. She was not married but had just started coming back to church and was trying to get her life back together when someone for whom she had tremendous respect approached her and incredulously made the comment, "YOU have a BABY!?" and then walked away without another word. The comment (probably made in total surprise and disbelief) did nothing to further that unwed mother's efforts in attending church at the time and made her feel as if the whole church thought badly of her. It took a long time for that unwed mother to get over that initial rejection and an even longer time for her to feel any part of the church—simply because she felt that everyone had those same thoughts. She now knows that the lady who made the comment was just surprised and made a thoughtless comment, but it still left a scar. She learned that God accepted her in spite of her past.

Has someone hurt your feelings without really meaning to? It could be in a passing comment or playing a game. What can you do? You cannot do anything about the person who hurt you, but you can turn to God and ask Him to heal your wounded spirit. *"Trust in him at all times...pour out your heart before him...."* (Psalm 62:8) You can counsel with a leader with whom you enjoy spending time and who enjoys spending time with you or with a good friend who knows what to say and do to help mend your feelings.

I read recently that part of growing up is being content with who you are and being strong enough to withstand any criticism. I was asked once how I was able to "win" my husband with the smile I wore (meaning I did not have a smile on my face at the time). It made me feel like I should not have been a part of what everyone else was doing at the time. I wanted to walk out. But when I heard that, I tried to determine if God liked what He saw or if it was something that I really did need to correct.

I can't imagine that there is anything more hurtful than a teen's being rejected by his parents. As I am out in public places, I often see a parent yelling at his children and even calling them names. As a youth director's wife, every once in a while I hear of someone who can't get along with Mom or Dad. (Usually it's one or the other—not both.) Sometimes it has to do with the way the teen treats his parents, and sometimes it truly is a matter of the teen's feeling rejected.

In the Bible you, as the child, are commanded to honor and obey your parents. Your mom and dad are not told to "be nice." You are to do what's right so that *"...it may be well with thee...."* (Ephesians 6:3) I think you'll find that if you concentrate more on what God wants of you, that feeling of rejection will at least take a back seat in your life and make life easier at home.

What about being rejected for doing right? In Luke 6:22 and 23 the

Bible says, "*Blessed are ye...for, behold, your reward is great in heaven....*" As much as "religious freedom" is argued about in our country, there are some who have been and will be rejected for standing for right. Believe it or not, this even happens in Christian schools. I heard a sermon recently about the number **one**. **One** person can make a difference. You can make a difference in maybe only one other person's life, but it's a difference. Take it as a personal challenge and take the stand even knowing it might bring you rejection.

It's so easy to just tuck ourselves away when we've been rejected by someone. It seems that the more people (friends, teachers, family) you have in your life and the more that you love and admire them, the more you open yourself up to rejection. I mean, do you really feel rejected when a complete stranger at the mall gives you a weird look for the way that you're dressed or makes a comment behind your back? No! You're not looking for that person's acceptance; you are looking for the acceptance of the people you feel are important to you.

Now, in spite of the fact that someone has rejected you, there should be a desire to reconnect with that person. Psalm 51 :10 says, "*Create in me a clean heart, O God; and renew a right spirit within me.*" I still had a desire to connect with my teachers. I knew there were probably things I still needed to learn from them. God had given me those teachers for a reason—to glean what knowledge I could from them.

I have a newspaper clipping in one of my drawers that reads, "Be sure to expose yourself to criticism: a fine polish requires an abrasive." Many times I take out that card, look at it, and then just smile because I think that the person who just hurt me was my abrasive. They are making me a stronger, more polished Christian. (Who knows? Maybe if those people knew that I thought they were MY abrasive, they would stop being so unkind.)

Lastly, as we deal with rejection in our own lives, it's just as important for us to remember not to make someone else feel rejected because of us. I pray that the girls in our youth group are never hurt or made to feel rejected by something I do or say. I love all of them. In I Corinthians 10:31, I'm reminded to "*...do all to the glory of God.*" That means the words and actions that I use each day are all supposed to be for God's glory, and in that case, I have to be careful what I say and do. I have to pray often for God to give me sweet words and thoughts because I don't always feel very sweet.

My mom used to tell me to think before I spoke so that I wouldn't hurt someone with careless words. Being aware of other people in all manner of speaking is one of the best rules to live by. Psalm 19: 14 says, *"Let the words of my mouth, and the meditation of my heart, be acceptable in thy sight, O LORD, my strength, and my redeemer."*

CHAPTER FOUR

The Beauty of Boldness

by Joy Jorgensen

The day had finally come. After nine months of preparation and prayer, your parents welcomed their first little girl. Cute pink dresses, little bows in her hair, and adorable tiny purses are just some of the ideas they had floating through their heads. However, as the years pass by, for this same little girl who is now a teenager to be a godly

David and Joy Jorgensen

and pure "princess," she must possess a quality that doesn't seem to carry much beauty to its name. She must have boldness. Yes, she must be fearless, courageous, and brave.

The statistics are frightening. Almost any type of research about teenagers today reveals that they are succumbing to peer pressure at an alarming rate. These are not all of the issues facing teenagers today, but here are some:

- Depression
- Anorexia
- Ungodly music
- Smoking
- Alcohol
- Drug abuse
- Cutting and hurting their own bodies
- Physical abuse
- Immorality

We can all look at this list and tell ourselves that these types of problems are only faced in the public school system, but they are not. In our Christian schools and in our church families, sad to say, these problems exist. The only possible way for a teenager to stand against these wiles of the Devil is to do just that—stand. We must have a boldness about us.

Many times in the New Testament, we can read and find examples of Christians exhibiting this needed trait. Maybe the most famous of verses about boldness is found in Hebrews 4:16 which states, "*Let us therefore come boldly unto the throne of grace, that we may obtain mercy, and find grace to help in time of need.*" If only I could transfer the heart and mind of a 29-year-old young adult to the heart and mind of a teen girl. This verse alone could complete the cure for each of the problems printed in the preceding list. Here are several steps to being that bold, courageous, and brave young lady:

1. Develop a life that makes you love and long for God. I did not say have a walk with God each day, although that is important. I did not say read your Bible and pray every morning, although you should. When Hebrews 4:16 speaks of coming boldly to the throne of grace, there is a power in that statement that still humbles the greatest of Christians. There will be days, weeks, months, and maybe years of your life when nothing will help you in your time of need except for grace.

As a teenage young lady, you do and will face temptations that sometimes seem impossible to withstand. On a daily basis you will face friends, and unfortunately sometimes even family, who want you to do something for the very first time that has been ingrained in you as wrong since childhood. A boy will want you to prove your love for him in an unholy manner. A family member will show you how to "relieve" stress and bitterness by cutting yourself and defaming the temple of the Holy Ghost.

It is at these crossroads in your life that you must, I repeat, you must have **already** secured a life that makes you love and long for God. You, on your own, are not strong enough to defeat the Devil, who wants your life permanently stained with sin. You need help. God, in His amazing grace, can provide this help. You are not in this battle alone. Whether you are the only one in your family who attends church or whether you are the pastor's kid, God is your best Friend. You must create a boldness of going to Him.

Hebrews 10:19 says, *"Having therefore, brethren, boldness to enter into the holiest by the blood of Jesus."* Too often Christians and especially teenagers use the excuse that they have no relationship with God because they are too sinful. You feel like God wants nothing to do with you because of your past or current behavior. What you don't understand is that you could not be further from the truth. God wants to hear from you. If you never talk to someone, it is very difficult to have a relationship with that person.

On the other hand, if you spend hours a day with someone, are always talking to that one, and you share your dreams and problems with him, you will feel very close to that person. It is no different with God. Making Him your closest friend will help in your time of need. Also, when your relationship with someone is strong, you are less likely to hurt that person because of the love you have developed for Him. Be bold in entering His presence. Tell God your fears, tell Him your battles, and tell Him you love Him—no matter how sinful or how unqualified to talk to Him you think you are. Talk to Him in the morning, in the afternoon, and in the evening. Please do not be fearful of your greatest ally.

One of the greatest lies Satan uses against a teenager is to tell him God does not love him and wants nothing to do with him because of who he is and what he has done. It takes great strength to say "no" to today's temptations facing you as a teenager. You can be bold, courageous, and brave. Stand against the Devil's lies by creating a love and a longing for God.

Have you ever been nervous about a job interview? Were you scared about an appointment with the principal? Could you even imagine getting to meet one-on-one with President Bush for an hour? Although it is hard for any human to comprehend, we have direct access to an all-present, all-knowing, and all-powerful God. He has the power to send anything in your life at any time, but He also has the power to provide any amount of grace at any time. What a promise God gives us in Hebrews 10:19. You may be fearful, as we should be, about entering His presence, but God still tells us to enter His holy presence with boldness.

Why is this possible? Because when we come to God and we tell Him all of our feelings and our thoughts, when we are in a problem and we feel there is no way out, we only have to call on God and claim that it's through the blood—the blood that Jesus shed on that Cross that covers all those things you tell yourself are in the way and keep you from being able to run to His side. It's through the blood that you can come boldly to His throne—yes, His wonderful throne where you will find more grace than you can possibly imagine.

2. **Determine that your personality will not hinder you.** One of the examples of boldness in the New Testament is found in Acts 4:13. *"Now when they saw the boldness of Peter and John, and perceived that they were unlearned and ignorant men, they marvelled; and they took knowledge of them, that they had been with Jesus."* When I was in junior high and high school, I was pretty reserved, unless I was with people I knew well. Yet people would tell me and have told me that I am a very bold soul winner. Just because you are on the quieter side or maybe not as popular as the next person, that has nothing to do with whether or not you will be able to be bold as a Christian. According to this text, Peter and John were not the smartest of men, nor did they even know how to speak to people well. However, people looked to them for leadership and learned from them simply because of their time with Jesus and the boldness that resulted from it. Acts 4:13 explains that everyone around them could plainly see it.

Once your life with Christ is firmly developed, boldness will in turn fall into place. Time with God will give you a boldness to say no to the friend who wants you to listen to the wrong music or watch the wrong movies. Time alone with God will give you a boldness not to chat online with people you have no business being online with at any time. Once you have been with Jesus, people will notice. People will marvel at the fact that you, no matter what your personality, popularity, or background in life, possess the power to boldly stand for what is right.

A young lady who feels her personality keeps her from taking a stand for right is in very serious trouble. Allow the Bible and your love of God to influence those around you. Determine that your personality will not hinder you, but it will make others marvel at the boldness God has given you.

3. **Daily prepare yourself for the individual battles and tests of boldness.** There is a well-known story of a girl who stood to sing "Stand Up, Stand Up, for Jesus" in the middle of a crowd of people listening to a speaker defy God. That young girl's boldness caused the crowd to join her in singing while the defiant atheist sneaked out of the room. On a daily basis though, more teenage girls' lives are ruined because they fail to boldly stand up to one person. Yes, it takes courage. Yes, it takes strength, but for your sake and the sake of those people you are supposed to help in the future, I beg you to daily prepare yourself.

When someone tells you to cut yourself, it is usually not in front of 300 people. Usually it is in a bedroom—just you and your "best friend." When someone hands you a glass of beer or suggests you listen to wrong music because she says it will make you feel good, relax, and forget all the people in your life that mistreat you—usually it will not be while you're sitting next to your parents in church. Usually it is alone, in a corner, where no one can see, except God.

Your parents and teen leaders can and will continue to warn you to not hang with the wrong crowd. They can also tell you to stay completely away from so and so, but the time will come when one on one you are tempted. It is very true that you should adhere to your parents' and leaders' advice as to whom not to spend time with, but one day you will face a temptation that you never saw coming. You might be at work when a co-worker invites you over to her house for a day that will ruin the rest of your life. These tests will come. The question is, will you have the boldness to stand for what is right? Are you going to right now determine that as a result of your love and longing for God that you will boldly stand for Christ? Will you also prepare for that battle tomorrow? Will you daily prepare for the individual times when Satan tries to make you one more statistic that we read about in the newspaper?

It may sound more fun and exciting to be like the girl in the illustration, to stand up in front of everyone and be the one person who claims to love God. Most likely though, given the normal everyday happenings, your turn for your boldness to "kick in" will simply come in front of one or two of your close friends—not in some great coliseum where you will be the hero, admired and used as an example for years to come. Will you be ready? There is no one who, on her own, can stand up against a friend or even a family member and boldly say "no" to something wrong. We need the help that God offers us. Daily prepare yourself for those individual battles.

4. Decide to put boldness into your conversations and into soul winning. Acts 4:31 says, *"And when they had prayed, the place was shaken where they were assembled together; and they were all filled with the Holy Ghost, and they spake the word of God with boldness."* This verse is very convicting to me for two reasons. First, I want to challenge each teen girl to put Christ in her conversation. Why are we so afraid of telling our friends what we received in our Bible this morning? As a Christian, wouldn't it make sense to talk about Him? It is sad that we see our friends for seven to ten hours a day at school, yet we only discuss who slept with whom on television the night before. We only talk about which singer divorced which actor yesterday and other issues that should never even be discussed. Let's bring Christ back into our conversation and boldly stand for Him.

Secondly, if we were to truly fill ourselves with the Holy Ghost, as Acts 4:31 states, soul winning would never be an issue. If our prayer life was anywhere close to this verse, then each trip to the mall or every contact with a neighbor would result in our witnessing to them. If we loved God like He loves us, then spreading the Gospel would be like a vacation that our families take in the summertime! Of course this does not happen because it is humanly impossible for us to even come close to loving Him the way He loves us, but we can strive every day to get closer to that goal.

It is of course very wise for you to study, prepare, and memorize verses that will aid you in the process of leading someone to Christ, but a bold Christian will be a witness anytime and anywhere. It is only our pride that prevents us from telling others about that trip to Calvary. May we love Him enough to humble ourselves and boldly tell others about Him.

Take a moment to realize what boldness could do for you. Do you fear approaching someone to tell them about the very God Who saved you from Hell? Do you fear what temptations may come upon you? Do you fear coming to Jesus because of all your shortcomings and mistakes? The beauty of boldness is not seen when you are at the door of an unsaved person. The beauty of boldness is not seen at the time of temptation. The beauty of boldness is not seen on a daily basis as you work to privately build a relationship with your Saviour.

The beauty of boldness is seen by all when you have a love and longing for God that results in a continual friendship with Him, rather than a "duty" to get out of bed to read your Bible. It will be found at the wedding altar on the most beautiful day of your life. It is then that the boldness you have developed through your teen years will be the reason why you have stood strong through the Devil' s attacks and will give you the right to marry a strong, godly Christian man. Today, please start developing a boldness about God to others.

CHAPTER FIVE

Have a Cabinet of Counselors

by Annie Lutz

David and Annie Lutz

———

Until I was 21, my life was fairly predictable. No huge disasters had taken place in my life. I was attending Hyles-Anderson College, had my group of friends, worked at a good steady job, and attended a church that I loved. My home life was ideal with two parents and a brother who loved me. However, my life began to drastically change during a summer college class at Hyles-Anderson College.

I was single and only interested in completing my degree. I was taking as many college classes as were allowed during a summer, and my focus was only on how many credits I could complete in as short a time as possible. I met Joe* during one of these classes. We sat next to each other, but I hadn't noticed him until he offered to help me by carrying a class project out to my car one day. He was what many girls looked for in a guy. He was tall, had dark hair, could sing, could make any girl laugh, was very talented, smart, and physically strong.

However, many men at Hyles-Anderson College are polite and courteous, so I wasn't sure what his motives, if any, were. But as I soon realized, he was interested in dating me. The next eight months was a whirlwind of dates, trips to meet his parents, sunsets at the dunes, and multiple phone calls. I was flooded with love notes, flowers, dinners at

———

* Not his real name

work, and other tokens of love. I was completely happy and even more thrilled when he told me he loved me and then asked me to become his wife. I had not pictured myself getting married so young, but I was happy with whom I thought the Lord had given me. Through all this, I maintained a close relationship with my parents and advisors, and nothing seemed wrong or gave us cause to be concerned.

Everything was perfect until one evening after church, my dad asked if he and my mom could take me for a ride. We drove around in silence for a while until my dad parked the car, turned to me, and with tears in his eyes said, "Baby, I'm about to break your heart." My father proceeded to tell me that Joe had been lying to me throughout our entire dating relationship. He had been completely untrue to me and to the morals I thought we both were trying to live by. Our entire future together was based on Joe's lies, and the life that he was living was something I could not be a part of. I learned that the man with whom I had fallen so quickly in love had been morally unfaithful to me.

I was crushed. What he told me did break my heart, and suddenly my perfect world came crashing down on top of me. I began to cry and could literally feel my heart falling apart. Inside I was screaming and trying so desperately to pick up the now fallen pieces, but nothing was working. Even as my dad was talking to me, all I could do was cry and think of how that the man and the world that I loved so much was now over. I did hear my dad ask me what I wanted at that exact moment, and I asked to be taken to the home of Brother and Mrs. Jack Schaap.

At this time, Brother Schaap was the vice president of Hyles-Anderson College, and the relationship that our family held with his was close. I had spent many counseling sessions with Brother Schaap and trusted him as a dear family friend and counselor. That night I, along with my parents and Brother and Mrs. Schaap, sat around their kitchen table as Brother Schaap gently guided me and my parents through what was happening and how our lives would be very difficult throughout the next few months.

Looking back now, I am so happy and grateful for parents who loved me enough to push me toward good, godly counselors and encouraged me to seek their advice. My life changed drastically that night, and at the time, I was sure that nothing was ever going to erase the pain and hurt I felt. I was able to receive counsel not only from Brother and Mrs. Schaap, but also from my parents who were forever strong and guided me as I grasped my way back into reality and the new life that was handed to me. I was also able to meet with my pastor, Dr. Jack Hyles, who tenderly loved me and my family and guided us down a new road and path which was to be my life.

Over the next 30 days, I experienced a barrage of events that still bring back sad memories and even tears. In 30 days I lost my fiancé; my hero, my friend, and my pastor of 21 years, Dr. Jack Hyles, was taken to Heaven; my dad learned he had to have open heart surgery; we moved from the home in which I had lived for 21 years; one of my best friends passed away; and I lost over 25 pounds. In the midst of these 30 dark days, however, I was able to graduate from college and held on to a strong relationship with my parents and counselors. As I tried to get my life back on track, I kept a close walk with God through my Bible reading and prayer. I continued to seek advice from my parents and Dr. and Mrs. Schaap, who by now had become my new pastor and pastor's wife.

My life started looking brighter when Dr. Schaap offered me a job at the church as a secretary to Dr. Eddie Lapina. I had grown up under the ministry of Brother Eddie and was thrilled to be on his staff. I decided to make myself useful and spent my evenings and weekends devoted to the church and its work. I helped with every activity, every soul-winning event, and was always available for anything that needed attention. I fell into a pattern which consisted of work and church and was content with the new life that I was making for myself. I wasn't dating and had absolutely no interest in pursuing anyone or having anyone pursue me. I had made a vow to never allow myself to be open and susceptible to the pain that I had experienced only a few short months before.

I was forced into yet another new phase when Dr. Schaap called me into his office and told me that I needed to start dating again. I instantly began to cry and told him this was completely impossible. Nevertheless, he told me that he was sending me someone to date, and when approached, I was to be nice and sweetly accept. I unwillingly followed his advice and began to date around. At no time was there anything that happened to me that I did not tell my parents or Dr. Schaap. My counselors remained strong in my life and were always there to help me.

During this time I started to really think about what I wanted and needed in a future husband. Having been engaged and so close to marriage and now unattached again, I wanted to make sure my priorities were in order and that I had a good solid relationship with my parents and my counselors. I began repeating Proverbs 3:5 and 6 over and over again in my head and out loud. *"Trust in the LORD with all thine heart; and lean not unto thine own understanding. In all thy ways acknowledge him, and he shall direct thy paths."* I completely believed in what these verses say; in that, if I sought after godly counsel and what God wanted in all my daily decisions, then He would guide and lead me to the road in which I would live my life and eventually to my future husband. I constantly worked to do what I felt Jesus wanted me to do and trusted that He would one day open my heart again and lead me to my future husband. It didn't happen overnight, nor was it a quick decision that never left me. It was a conclusion I had to come to in realizing that I was done trying to do things "my way" and needed God's help in order for my life to truly be complete by finding and doing God's perfect will for my life. I realized that I couldn't spend all my time wondering whom I was going to marry or asking myself why God had not brought "Mr. Right" into my life. I could only trust Jesus completely, follow what I felt He wanted me to do, and trust that He would take care of me in His perfect time, and He did!

One evening while I was waiting for the church service to begin, my friend Jaclynn (Schaap) Weber approached me and told me she had the perfect guy for me to date. Now Jaclynn and I have been friends our entire lives, and if I considered anyone to be like my sister, it was Jaclynn. So, I was fairly surprised when she said this because she knew what I had been through and how I was handling everything. Nonetheless, I said I would meet David, this "perfect guy."

I did meet David and right away noticed how good looking and athletically built he was. He was tall, a great dresser, and his smile completely melted my heart. I was very impressed with him, but we began our relationship as just friends. Over time we began to spend more time together as he settled in at Hyles-Anderson College that fall.

Our church had an annual Red Cross blood drive, and that year I had volunteered to help. David came to give blood, but before he was taken in line, we sat down together and began to talk. I realized that this friend I had was very interesting and incredibly handsome and that I was very much wanting to be more than friends! He finally had to leave to give blood but promised me that we would talk again. He kept his promise, and we began to date each other regularly. I soon realized that the good dates I had had with Joe were nothing compared to the fun I was having with David. The times David and I shared together were far better and more meaningful than anything I had experienced with Joe. David began to love me in a way that far exceeded anything I thought was ever possible. David showed me what was real and honest and what it felt like to be loved and taken care of by a man. He truly was my perfect guy!!

Not forgetting my priorities, I sought the advice of my parents and my counselors. After spending more time with David, I realized that I loved him and was designed to be his help meet. Both he and I had many counseling sessions with our parents and counselors and did not make any decisions until we felt like it was certainly God's will for both our lives.

Now five years later, David and I are happily married and have a beautiful daughter. I am so thankful I trusted in both my parents and godly counsel in the decisions I made regarding dating and marrying my husband. Without them, I would not have the man or marriage God designed for me to have. Before any of this happened to me, I had always heard that having a "cabinet of counselors" was wise, and I knew the Bible said in Proverbs 11:14, *"Where no counsel is, the people fall: but in the multitude of counsellors there is safety."* However, everything became more real to me when I was forced to realize that these statements were indeed true and that my life would only matter when I gave it over to Jesus and let Him guide me.

CHAPTER SIX

Preparing for the Real World
by Trina Reynolds

I once heard a story about an elderly lady who lived alone. Although she was extremely poor, she would pay for water to be delivered to her home once a week. Even the delivery man wondered why she would pay such a high price for water when she could get water much cheaper from the city. Finally one day he asked her, "Ma'am, why do you pay for me to deliver water every week?"

"Sir," she answered, "I'll pay any price to have someone come and greet me once a week."

David and Trina Reynolds

This story is so sad to me, but I have to wonder what relationship(s) in life she had not worked on. There are so many lonely people in this world, but it never has to be you. You can prepare now for your future to live a happy, prosperous life with no regrets. These are just a few ideas to help you.

Seek God First

Seek God for the big things. Matthew 6:33 says, *"But seek ye first the kingdom of God, and his righteousness; and all these things shall be added unto you."* Many girls are seeking for the "these things" that they want out of life without first seeking God. They want the immediate gratification today instead of a lifetime of joy God's way.

Schedule your time with God. Everything important in life is scheduled. Your school, job, dentist appointments, dates, etc. all are scheduled. The ONE Who can give you the most blessed life is not always scheduled. Some girls want that boyfriend now, and yes, they can have some immediate happiness; or they can wake up and spend time with God and allow Him to give them a man with a great marriage to last a lifetime.

Start by praying and reading your Bible just a few verses each day. It only takes five minutes CONSISTENTLY to start your walk with God. Many can say that they read the Bible, but few can say that they read it every day. Ask yourself, "What will I lose if I don't, or what will I gain if I do?" Pray about your future while preparing for it. Learn to treat God like He is right next to you when you wake up, because He is.

I heard of a high school boy who never read his Bible. One day he heard a chapel speaker give his testimony and encourage the students to read one verse a day. He said that he didn't remember anything else about the testimony, but he felt that he could go home and read one verse. The first night he read one verse and thought it was quite easy. He started adding more and more verses each day. Finally it became nothing for him to read chapters every day. He ended up attending Hyles-Anderson and will soon be marrying a great girl. He surely is happy that he didn't waste his life being depressed and trying to live his life by himself. It started with reading only one verse a day.

Don't look at your Bible as a chore. Make it your fun time with God. During this past summer my daughters have loved using a children's devotional book written by Robin Ogle entitled *This Is the Day!: The Adventures of Sheriff Ogle and His Deputies.* She includes a verse to ponder on all day and a truth to help you. Plus, she makes it fun to have a relationship with God. You can't expect to have a good future if you don't put God in it today. Micah 6:8 says, *"He hath shewed thee, O man, what is good; and what doth the Lord require of thee, but to do justly, and to love mercy, and to walk humbly with thy God?"*

Seek God in the little things each day. Proverbs 3:5-6 says, *"Trust in the LORD with all thine heart; and lean not unto thine own understanding. In all thy ways acknowledge him, and he shall direct thy paths."* Now that you pray and read your Bible daily, put Him in the little things of life. Take a verse you read each day and apply it to your life. Ask Him what to wear, who to help, what to buy, what classes to take, etc. Bringing God into the little decisions of your life gives you more of a heart for

God. You must make Him your God, not just the God of your parents and pastor.

While dating in college, I had an argument with my boyfriend and afterward read Psalm 141:3, *"Set a watch, O Lord, before my mouth; keep the door of my lips."* From then on I knew I had to pray for God's control over my tongue. Oftentimes we think to pray about the big matters in our lives and frequently overlook the seemingly little ones; the tongue is one of those areas.

My husband and I pray for the right parking spot and our seat at a restaurant. Our lives are much more peaceful when we allow God to be a part of everything.

You must learn now how to cultivate a heart for God and put Him in your daily life so that you truly value Him. Do not wait for a trial or heartache to want Him in your life.

God uses means that some would call unfair to accomplish His will and to draw us closer to Him. We are not the main objective; God's will is the main objective.

I remember telling God how good He was in my life. Then my first husband died, and I thought, "Did I truly mean 'God is good' when I said it?" Valuing God now helps you walk through your trials. Be now what you want to become in the future.

Read your Bible, pray, love God, and love others like you want to be loved.

Learn How to Work Hard

Build your character daily. Deuteronomy 24:19c says, *"...that the Lord thy God may bless thee in all the work of thine hands."* Make yourself now get up at the same time every day. My daughters follow the same schedule on spring break and even in the summer. I want to prepare them for life. When I want to complain about the work I have to do, I try to picture myself with a sickness or even paralyzed and unable to work.

It is amazing how your outlook on work changes when you think of people you know who don't have that privilege. As a mother, you can't sleep in when your baby is crying and needs you. Your husband might need breakfast at 6:00 a.m., but if you have told yourself that you can't make it unless you sleep in, then you will not be what your husband needs. As a wife and mother, your work is not only from 8:00 to 5:00. It is around the clock, and it is the greatest job in the world. Also, children are work, so if you don't learn to love work and to do the jobs that aren't always enjoyable, then you will have a hard time enjoying your children. As a mother, you will work even when you are on vacation.

If you want to promote righteousness in your life, work on your responsibilities. If you want to promote anger, talk about your rights. For women especially, we are told more about our rights than our responsibilities. Through college I would hear girls speak about what kind of man they were looking to marry, yet I never heard what preparations they were making to become a good wife. Living by your feelings produces failures; living to fulfill your responsibilities produces great feelings. God will give you your rights if you take care of your responsibilities. The closer you walk with God, the more power He gives you do what seems hard to you.

Prepare Now to Be a Good Wife.

1. **Read good books.** Read books on organization, loving others, dating, cookbooks, biographies, etc. I am sure your pastor's wife would have a good list to start with.

2. **Go soul winning or visit a shut-in.** We all can benefit from thinking about someone else's future.

3. **Learn how to cook and bake well.** Take a cooking class or work with someone who can cook. Every boy wants to marry a girl who can cook. I believe in the statement, "The way to a man's heart is through his stomach."

4. **Practice good hygiene.** My mom used to say, "No one is too poor to buy a bar of soap." You will always be proud of yourself for being clean and smelling good.

5. **Eat healthy and exercise.** I didn't eat perfect through my teen years, but I did try to work on it. My mother is a very petite lady, and I have watched her for years eat very few sweets and not eat after 7:00 in the evening. You need to exercise every week. Not just for your weight,

but also for your heart and other organs. It would be great even if you just jog on a mini-trampoline for twenty minutes four times a week. Even ten minutes a day would be worthwhile.

    6. Listen to good music and sing often. Listening often to good music helps your mind not wonder and worry about things that either don't matter or should be given to the Lord. You must learn now how to control your mind.

    7. Learn how to clean your house well and on a schedule. When I married at the age of 20, I scheduled to clean my house every Monday. After my husband passed away, I cleaned my house the following Monday. My schedule helped me to not go insane some days. I knew what I was going to do when I woke up. Being a hard worker builds your confidence. Even when my two-year-old son starts misbehaving, I just put him to work in order to bring a big smile on his face.

    You have a sense of accomplishment when you complete a task. If you don't build your confidence through work, why should others have confidence in you. One of my husband's favorite sayings is, "God has used every type of sinner in the Bible, but he has never used a lazy man."

Learn Now to Be Grateful

    I Thessalonians 5:18 says, *"In every thing give thanks: for this is the will of God in Christ Jesus concerning you."* Gratefulness is the foundation of our walk with God and of His daily will for our lives. We must give thanks for everything, including heartaches, sickness, criticism from others, and whatever trials happen to us.

    Thankfulness is the best medicine to not get depressed. Depression is a form of selfishness. If we start feeling discouraged or depressed, we must get alone and start thanking God for each and every thing that we have. Realize that all we deserve is Hell, but Jesus saved us and is giving us a life filled with blessings. Take your mind off of your problems and think about how much God loves you. This is why telling others about Jesus is more than just a command. It is a way to show that we are truly grateful for what God has done for us. **No matter what we think we deserve, nothing will make us as happy as being grateful.**

    1. Thank God each morning for a new day. Psalm 118:24 says,

"This is the day which the Lord *hath made; we will rejoice and be glad in it."*

2. Thank God for Heaven and for saving your soul. James 1:17a says, *"Every good gift and every perfect gift is from above...."*

3. Thank God for His mercies. Thank Him that they are new every morning. Lamentations 3:22, 23 says, *"It is of the* Lord's *mercies that we are not consumed, because his compassions fail not. They are new every morning: great is thy faithfulness."*

4. Thank God for your health—good or bad. Psalm 119:71 states, *"It is good for me that I have been afflicted; that I might learn thy statutes."* I hardly ever became sick until my husband passed away. I did not think God should allow me to get sick after taking my husband. I finally started to focus on what I had and to be grateful for it. I believe God allowed me to get sick so that when I felt better, I would have a renewed energy and appreciation to take care of my girls. Helen Keller said, "So much has been given to me, I have no time to ponder over that which has been denied."

5. Thank God for something in your life that you normally take for granted and praise Him for it. Psalm 92:1 says, *"It is a good thing to give thanks unto the* Lord, *and to sing praises unto thy name, O most High."*

I heard about a man who had been beaten and robbed. He came home to his family and said, " I was beat up, but not killed. I was robbed, but I am not the one who robbed." It is all in the way we control our minds and about what we decide to think.

I know we all have areas to work on. It just takes a balance to work on the most important relationships we have. REMEMBER: WHAT YOU DO DAILY IS WHAT YOU BECOME PERMANENTLY.

CHAPTER SEVEN

Living by Faith

by Ashley Richards

Faith of our Fathers! living still
In spite of dungeon, fire, and sword:
O how our hearts beat high with joy
When-e'er we hear that glorious word!

Faith of our Fathers! holy faith!
We will be true to thee 'till death!

Faith of our fathers, we still strive
To win all nations unto thee!
And thro' the truth that comes from God
Mankind shall then indeed be free.

Jason and Ashley Richards

Faith of our fathers! holy faith!
We will be true to thee 'till death!

Faith of our fathers! we will love
Both friend and foe in all our strife:
And preach thee, too, as love knows how,
By kindly words and virtuous life:

Faith of our fathers! holy faith!
We will be true to thee 'till death!

When I take the time to read and really think about the words of this song, I am reminded of how blessed I am. This song is referring to the martyrs of the sixteenth century who were persecuted, sometimes tortured for their faith.

The songwriter is paying tribute to the men and women who, in spite of dungeon, fire, and sword, stayed true to their faith and their God. Since the beginning of time to present day, people have been and are still being persecuted for what they believe. We are so blessed to live in a free country that enables us to worship how we desire. We might at some time have to stand alone for what we believe or suffer some minor embarrassment, maybe even sever a friendship. But torture? Prison? Not likely.

Faith is defined as "belief in, devotion to, or trust in somebody or something, especially without logical proof." The Bible describes faith as *"the substance of things hoped for, the evidence of things not seen."* There are many examples of great faith in the Bible.

- Hannah believed God would give her a son so much that her fervent prayer caused her to be mistaken for a drunk.
- Moses' mother had a great deal of faith to place her baby in the bulrushes and then to quietly watch as Pharaoh's daughter reared **her** son.
- Mary was a young, unmarried girl who had to have been scared when she found out she was carrying the seed of the Holy Ghost. Joseph had to have faith when the angel told him not to be afraid, but to take Mary as his wife.
- Abraham was ready to sacrifice his only son. The Bible says Abraham had faith that God would raise Isaac from the dead after he was sacrificed. *"By faith Abraham, when he was tried, offered up Isaac: and he that had received the promises offered up his only begotten son, Of whom it was said, That in Isaac shall thy seed be called: Accounting that **God was able to raise him up, even from the dead**; from whence also he received him in a figure."* (Hebrews 11:17-19)

"For unto whomsoever much is given, of him shall be much required: and to whom men have committed much, of him they will ask the more." (Luke 12:48) I am compelled, by how much I have been given, to live for God and to pass on what I have learned to my children. If you did not grow up in a Christian home or have the opportunity to attend a Christian school supported by a wonderful church with a pastor and people who loved and cared for you as I did, you have still been "given much." The

Bible says, "...*yea, I have a goodly heritage.*" Galatians 3:26 tells us "*For ye are all the children of God by faith in Christ Jesus.*" Once you are saved, you are a part of God's family. The men and women of faith in the Bible and the martyrs of the past and present are all a part of your Christian heritage.

When you have been saved at an early age and essentially "grow up in church," it is very easy to take the Christian way of life for granted, to just assume that because of who you are and where you attend church, you are in good standing with the Lord. We look at getting saved as simply something we should do to secure our eternity, rather than looking at it as the beginning of a wonderful lifelong relationship with our Saviour. Just as easy as it may be to mindlessly sing a great hymn of the faith without giving any thought to the words, we can "fake" the role of a Christian by outwardly conforming. You may appear to have it all together on the outside, but inside you are hollow, having never developed your own faith, your own **personal** relationship with the Lord.

On October 23, 1999, I married my high school sweetheart and my best friend, Jason Richards. When I said "I do," I was saying "I have faith in you, I trust you, I believe in you." That day was the beginning of our lifelong journey together. In each stage of our marriage, we find new ways to deepen our relationship to keep it strong. On my wedding day, I made a decision to forever bind my heart with Jason's; this is much like what happens when you get saved. You are deciding to take Jesus as your Saviour and put all your faith in Him. We need to work on our relationship with the Lord as we would work on a marriage relationship or any other relationship of value.

It takes time and commitment. When we really love someone, we want to please that person and honor him with what we say and do. If we say we love the Lord, then why is it so hard to decide to follow the path that He has designed for our lives? When we disobey our authorities and try to forge our own path in life, we are essentially saying we know better than those that have gone before us.

At some point in your life, you will have to decide what you believe in and why you believe it. Do you believe in God? Do you believe that the Bible is true? If so, do you believe that God's laws are meant for you?

Do you believe that a life of faith is worth living, no matter the sacrifice? Romans 3:3-4a, *"For what if some did not believe? shall their unbelief make the faith of God without effect? God forbid: yea, let God be true, but every man a liar...."*

You may never have to stand in front of a crowd of people and tell them what you believe in and why, but life will bring about circumstances that will cause you through your actions to tell the whole world what or who your faith is in. I want my faith to be in Jesus. I want my life to be a reflection of His wonderful grace and mercy. If my confidence is only in myself and what I can do, I will fail miserably. *"That your faith should not stand in the wisdom of men, but in the power of God."* (I Corinthians 2:5)

There are many accounts in the New Testament where Jesus healed people simply because they believed He could. In Matthew, Jesus tells His disciples if they have faith as a grain of mustard seed, they can move mountains; nothing shall be impossible.

Let's think about that. A mustard seed is pretty small, but a grain of a mustard seed is even smaller, and that much faith can move a mountain. How much faith then do we need to believe that God really does love us? He really does want the best for us. He really does want us to serve Him.

I don't know what the future holds for me or you. I do know that we have an awesome God Who is worthy of our love, our time, and our devotion. Whether we are asked to have the faith that could move a mountain or whether we just need the faith to get us through each day, God can supply it.

I want to challenge you to live a life of faith by daily asking the Lord to show you His plan for your life. The Bible is rich in promises for you. You will never be disappointed if you give your heart to Jesus. Decide that you will add to your already rich heritage by living in a way that pleases the Lord. Decide to have the faith of our fathers. *"As ye have therefore received Christ Jesus the Lord, so walk ye in him: Rooted and built up in him, and stablished in the faith, as ye have been taught, abounding therein with thanksgiving."* (Colossians 2:6, 7)

CHAPTER EIGHT

Building a Good Relationship with Your Siblings

by Candace Schaap

"A soft answer turneth away wrath: but grievous words stir up anger."
(Proverbs 15:1)

I grew up in a family of all girls. I am number four of the six. That's right, six girls—no boys! People would often say, "Oh, your poor dad!" But actually, between the emotional escapades, he was pretty spoiled, and if you will allow me to say this, girls, please spoil your dad! Comb his hair, rub his feet (as smelly as they might be), and when you are baking cookies for your boyfriend, make sure you make some for your dad. Just make him feel loved. Your dad sacrifices a lot to make you happy; you can sacrifice a few minutes of your busy day to take care of him. (That was all free!)

Ken and Candace Schaap

Now, with six girls you can imagine what our house was like. Just think of everything that you have gone through as a woman and multiply that by six, and that's my family. We had every personality imaginable. We all look very much alike, but we are as different as night and day. We have changed quite a bit as we have gotten older, but when we were young, our personalities were very distinct.

My oldest sister Brooke was like the mother hen. She always took care of us. She was never bossy—just caring and sweet. She would cook and clean for us, help us with homework and school projects, and was kind of quiet but extremely thoughtful of others. It was very hard to set Brooke off about anything.

Then there was Ashley, number two. Ashley was a tomboy and involved in everything. Ashley was very outgoing, talkative, and mischievous. She probably got into more trouble for pulling pranks than all the rest of us put together.

Heather was also very outgoing, but at home she could be antagonistic. She would do things on purpose just to see if she could make one of us angry. Heather was also the most tenderhearted one. She was always very quick to apologize and to do something for you to make up. Heather watched out for you at school. She would "fight" anyone who didn't like one of her sisters. She was very protective.

I was very quiet and kept to myself. I was also a whiner, which got on everyone's nerves. I loved to be alone and was very honest and blunt. For instance, I always thought that surely my sisters would want someone to tell them if they were starting to look fat, but that seemed to cause a lot of problems too. (I can't imagine why!)

Amber was the complete opposite of me. She was feisty, yet lovable and fun. Amber is probably the craziest one. If you want to have a fun party, invite Amber. If you made Amber angry, however, she would come out swinging, and you would run for your life because she was quite strong. She can make you laugh until you cry, and she is also a very emotional person. One minute she is crying about something, and the next minute she is laughing hysterically about that same thing. She has a great spirit, and when I am down, I try to be around Amber.

Finally, the baby Tara is the brain of the family. She usually helped Amber with her homework. Tara was also the servant. When she was really little, she would run around and do anything for anyone. If you wanted a drink, you sent Tara. If you needed a shirt ironed, you asked Tara. She would brush your hair, rub your back—anything really. Poor thing, I think she just wanted to be with the big girls. You ask, "You really 'used' her like that?"

Well, "use" is a very strong word. Tara loved serving us. Who were we to stop her from her "calling" in life? Now she is reaping the benefits of being the baby of the family because the baby always gets spoiled. I really don't think she minds being the youngest anymore!

As you can see from my descriptions, we are all very different. And with our differences came disagreements, arguments, and plain old knockdown, drag-out fights. So I asked myself, "Why is it that we could fight so much and yet be the best of friends?" I came up with a few answers to that question that I believe might help other sisters (and even with brothers too).

1. We often fought with each other, but we always fought for each other. When I was in junior high, I guess a couple of girls didn't like me very much. We were all on the ballfield one day, and one them playfully started to push me a little. I just thought she was kidding, so I ignored it and backed up some. When one of them punched me in the arm and said she wanted to fight me, I became very afraid upon realizing the playful pushing was not in jest. The girl who was pushing me was much stronger and bigger than I. I clearly stated that I was not going to fight. They continued pushing me, trying to provoke me into fighting them.

While this was happening, someone had run and told my sister Heather that I was in a fight, so Heather and her friend ran out to the field and started letting those girls have it. Of course, this turn of events relieved me greatly, and I was excited about my chances now that I had been rescued. My excitement was short-lived, however, when I heard Heather say, "Just because Candace is a weenie doesn't mean you have to pick on her." (Calling me a "weenie" was the best she could do in defending me? It was nice to be defended, but she could have done a better job of describing me!)

We stood up for each other; we fought for each other. I know I can't completely stop you from fighting with your siblings at home, but at least leave those fights at home. When you are at school, on a trip, or at a birthday party, stand up for each other. Don't let other girls talk bad about your sisters. My dad always told me that when all of our friends had moved away and childhood sweethearts were long forgotten, we would still have our family, so we should continually do our best to maintain the bond with each other.

2. Our relationship with each other was more important than our relationship with our friends. I went through a period of time, specifically in my sophomore year of high school, where I really didn't have any friends. My best friends at the time were all involved in a program which took them away from school for many trips and left me alone in my classes. That year Heather and I became very close. I'm sure she just felt sorry for me, but she let me do everything with her. I would hang out with her and her friends and go different places, including special events they would have. I know it must have been annoying for her to have her little sister tagging along with her everywhere she went, but she had no idea what it did for me.

Heather never made me feel like I was an annoyance to her. She went out of her way to make me feel like I was just one of them. She was awesome. I had the best year of high school under what I thought were the worst circumstances all because Heather didn't care what her friends thought. It didn't matter if they didn't want me along; she brought me because her relationship with me was more important than her relationship with her friends. To this day, Heather and I are best friends because of a choice she made in high school.

3. We didn't take advantage of each other's weaknesses. Most of my years at home we lived in very tight quarters. At one point four of us were sharing a room. In the summer months we traveled as a family, crammed into either a van or a motorhome. So you can imagine how close we were and how well we knew each other.

One thing we loved to do together was sing. My sisters and I have been singing since we were very young. We started off singing for the sailors in the sailor ministry, and as we grew and our voices matured, we would sing in churches before our dad preached. Not the most phenomenal of singers, it took lots of hard work to get us to the point of sounding decent.

Practice for us began in the van at the beginning of the trip and continued until we arrived at our destination. Amber and Tara were still quite young at the time, so they didn't perform with us. This didn't stop them from trying to practice with us, which led to some hilarious-sounding music. Amber's loud, high-pitched squeals (she called it singing) didn't do much at all to improve our sound, so naturally the older girls would make fun of her, which would bring her to tears. Of course, our laughter, along with Amber's crying, would earn us a stern lecture from Dad. He would tell us that one day Amber would have the best voice of us all. I'm pretty sure God punished us for making fun of her because my dad was right. Amber has the most beautiful voice and can outsing us all.

Obviously we were not perfect, and many times one of us would slip and take something too far and hurt someone, but because we were so close and knew each other so well, we never took advantage of each other in public. Arguments we had stayed in the house, though we could have easily driven each other into the ground with hateful words, but we chose to protect each other.

I mentioned that we loved to sing. Unless all six of us are singing together, it never quite feels right. We could be in the middle of an argument, and if one of us started to sing, the arguing would go on hold while everyone joined in the chorus. We never were professional, and sometimes we probably sounded downright bad, but I think God gave us this ability to insure peace among ourselves.

We definitely had our hard times. (I still have the scar from when my sister burned me with the curling iron. She says it was an accident— liar!) We were and still are far from perfect, but somewhere along the road, our parents instilled in us a desire to stay close and love each other. As much as we sometimes hated being crammed into a van for three months out of the year, this is probably what helped us the most. We were forced to get along, and it definitely kept us humble. I realize that not everyone can travel together like my family had the joy of doing, but there are things you can do to build a good relationship with your siblings. If you will use these three principles, your relationship with your siblings will grow stronger.

• **Quit being so selfish.** Try putting someone else's needs before your own. Let your sister do her hair in the bathroom first, share your clothes, allow someone else to sit in the front seat of the car for once. One of my sisters used to claim that she got sick if she sat in the back seat, so she always had to sit in the front. (I'm pretty sure she was not telling the whole truth!) Girls, the day I realized I had six wardrobes instead of just one, sharing clothes became great!

- **Work, fun, and ministry were centered around our family.** Everything we did, we did together. My mom made sure our house was fun so our friends would want to come over. No one watches your child like you will, and this way my mom could watch us. We didn't know that's what she was doing; all we knew was that it was a lot of fun to be at home. Of course we were allowed to go on activities, school functions, and occasionally to a friend's house, but ultimately we wanted to be at home. You will love those with whom you spend time and those with whom you serve. That's life.

- **Love is a choice and an act of the will.** Choose to love your sister or brother. I don't mean, "I love you, but I hate everything about you because everything you do irritates me." Look past the irritations and realize that your siblings have feelings too. Realize that sometimes the things you say leave scars that last forever. My sisters and I have the best relationship, and we are closer now than we have ever been because for us, relationships are more important than things or having our own way. Nothing is worth the cost of a relationship.

CHAPTER NINE

No Regrets with My Mom

by Deb Wilson

What an honor and a privilege to write about my wonderful mother, Mrs. Dorothy Paisley. When I was asked to address this subject, I jumped at the opportunity. Then I thought, "There are so many things to say about my wonderful mom! Where do I begin?"

Wes and Deb Wilson

One night as I woke up to feed my sweet baby Travis, I was thinking once again about this chapter and having no regrets with my mother. I could not go back to sleep after feeding Travis. This subject is such a wonderful one on which to dwell. The first thing that came to my mind was Galatians 5:22 and 23 which says, *"But the fruit of the spirit is love, joy, peace, longsuffering, gentleness, goodness, faith, Meekness, temperance: against such there is no law."* As my mind dwelt on those verses, I immediately thought of my mom. These verses describe my mother. Please allow me to show you how.

1. *Love*—"strong affection or liking for someone or something." My mother is full of love for her husband, her children, her grandchildren, her friends, and the people who attend her church, and yes, even strangers. I love the meaning of *love*—"strong affection or liking." I have always known that my mother likes me and loves me unconditionally, and I like her and love her unconditionally. She is always so full of love for everyone.

2. *Joy*—"a very glad feeling; happiness; delight." Wow! What a wonderful meaning! This is a perfect definition for my mom and our household as we grew up.

I remember when my dad would come home from working at the church. The minute he would walk in the door, my mom would say, "Daddy's home!" My sister, my mom, our dogs, and I would all greet Daddy at the door. He loved it, and we loved it right back. What a joy to grow up in the Paisley household.

3. *Peace*—"serenity, calm, or quiet." My mother has a peace about her. She was diagnosed with uterine cancer in August of 2004. Since that time, she has had to endure such trials through her illness. I have never heard her complain or question God through any of it because she has peace.

One of her favorite verses is Isaiah 26:3, which says, *"Thou wilt keep him in perfect peace, whose mind is stayed on thee: because he trusteth in thee."* My mom trusts in the Lord so much that she has perfect peace. When I have had very rough days, I know I can call my mom and she will give me verses to dwell on like Isaiah 26:3 because of her peace. She never gets "ruffled" over things that come into her life. Her favorite song is " 'Tis So Sweet to Trust in Jesus." She has lived this song.

4. *Longsuffering*—"bearing trouble." My mother had bus route #2 for over 20 years. Watching her with those precious bus kids, I could see that she was longsuffering. She would buy them groceries when their families had no food, she would bring some of the bus kids home with her on Sunday afternoon because their parents were not home when she tried to drop them off. Former bus kids recognize her and stop to tell her thank you. I believe it is longsuffering to care about others more than yourself.

5. *Gentleness*—"generous, kind, patient." I have always thought of my mother as being gentle. She is always a gentle person to everyone she meets whether or not that person is gentle.

Our family has always been animal lovers, and I remember my mom always taking in the stray dogs or just being gentle and loving to any animal. Her gentleness is amazing.

6. *Goodness.* "the state or quality of being good; virtue, kindness." *"Who can find a virtuous woman? for her price is far above rubies. The heart of her husband doth safely trust in her, so that he shall have no need of spoil. She will do him good and not evil all the days of her life."* (Proverbs 31:10-12)

These verses are a perfect example of what my mom is to my dad. I have never seen a better marriage in my life. They love each other. My mother is a virtuous woman, with amazing goodness, who has done my dad good and not evil by being a loving, kind wife to him, as well as living for him and her family.

7. *Faith*—"unquestioning belief in God; complete trust in confidence." My sister, Liz Rogers, and I recently made a CD of my mom's favorite songs. All of the songs she chose for us to sing talk about faith or trust in God. My mother has complete faith in God.

8. *Meekness*—"patient, mild, and submissive." All three of these meanings of meekness portray my mother and her life. She has been so patient through this whole trial of having cancer. She is a warrior in every sense of the word. All of my life I have watched how submissive my mom has been to my dad as well as to the other authorities in her life. She has never questioned what is asked of her.

9. *Temperance*—"self-restraint in conduct; moderation." My mom has always been very appropriate in her conduct with others. She is the best in dealing with people. She has a great sense of humor and a loving spirit toward others. She is a great teacher for her daughters, and we love and admire her very much.

I have no regrets with my mom. First of all, she and I have not only been mother and daughter, but we have also been friends. She is a wonderful mother to her children and a wonderful grandmother to her grandchildren.

The following are some ways that my mom and I are close:

- I try to call her or somehow talk to her every day.
- If I need help with something concerning motherhood, I ask her.
- What a wonderful example she was to me in being a great wife to my dad. I always ask her questions about that subject or seek advice from her about marriage.
- I pray for her every day. I believe the best gift you can give anyone is to pray for that person. I pray for my parents' health every day because I want my sister's children and my children to know our parents—their grandparents.

When I heard the words "Mom has cancer," nothing was ever the same again. The words were spoken, and this raging enemy entered our lives like a whirlwind. This is not a journey we would have chosen, but oh, the sweet moments the Shepherd has given along the way. His "whispers in the night" have sustained, comforted, and encouraged our hearts and reminded us that He is near.

Mom has battled cancer like a warrior in this fight for her life—in a fight to see her children become parents, to become a grandmother herself, and to continue to be the godly wife that she has been for over 44 years. In her family's eyes, Dorothy Paisley is a hero.

My parents,
John and Dorothy Paisley

CHAPTER TEN

The Highest Calling
by Leah Woosley

In today's society many look at a housewife as some poor, unfortunate soul who could not make it in the business world, so she is doomed to spend her days taking care of children and meeting the needs of her husband. Contrary to what today's society may tell you, I believe being a wife and mother is one of the highest callings to which a woman can be called. In the following paragraphs, I have listed several reasons why I believe being a wife and mother is the highest calling for me.

James and Leah Woosley

1. Being a wife and mother is the highest calling for me because it is God's will for my life. The Bible says in Romans 12:2, *"And be not conformed to this world: but be ye transformed by the renewing of your mind, that ye may prove what is that good, and acceptable, and perfect, will of God."* You prove the will of God by what you do. You prove what is important to you by what you do, not by what you say.

You need to be preparing now so that you may prove the will of God in your life to be good. You should be gathering information now to prove what is the good, acceptable will of God in the future by studying the Bible, praying, reading good Christian books, listening in church, and watching those marriages that you admire. You can be preparing to be a wife and mother by being submissive now to authority, serving others, obeying your parents, and getting along with others.

Sometimes we think being a wife and a mother will always be fun, happy, easy, and dreamy. The fact is, if you have a hard time getting along with your mom, dad, brothers, and sisters, you will have a hard time getting along with your husband and children someday. It takes patience, prayer, and a serving attitude to prove that being a wife and mother is God's will for your life.

2. Being a wife is the highest calling for me because I enjoy my husband. We enjoy each other's company. We have fun together. We enjoy sitting and talking to each other. I love doing things for him. I want to treat him like he is the most special person in the world because that's what he is to me. I want him to know, without my telling him, that I love him and trust him. I want him to know that he is thought about each day. I can do this by putting a note in the car, making a meal that he really enjoys, leaving a message on his cell phone, sending him a letter at work, and praying that he has a great day.

You can prepare to be a good wife today by practicing some things at home. Find needs to fill for your dad and mom. Stick letters in a pair of shoes or in their car. Buy them a special drink they like or write them appreciative notes. Pray for them. Find ways that you can make them feel special.

Allow me to share a powerful quote from Mrs. Schaap's book *A Wife's Purpose*. "The Devil most often destroys a man through a woman. The Devil most often destroys a woman through dissatisfaction." By being a servant and finding ways to love your husband (or for your parents and youth leaders now), you keep the Devil from creeping in and planting seeds of dissatisfaction. He does not want you to succeed at being a good daughter now or a good wife in the future. He wants to tear down your parents and your authorities now in your life. He wants you to think that you know what is best for yourself rather than those who are over you. He doesn't want you to be submissive; he wants you to think that submission is like being a slave and you won't get any glory; you will feel left out.

You need to be sure as a young Christian lady that you take the time it takes to get to know God. Reading your Bible, memorizing it, and praying are powerful tools to straighten out your thinking. See in the future what God has for you. For most of you, God will have a husband who needs a wife who loves him, trusts him, and is willing to do God's will. That husband needs someone who will let him do what he feels God has called him to do. Don't expect praise from others for being a great wife; learn to be happy with the fact that there is a God in Heaven Who is happy you are doing your best to do His will. Have joy in yourself, knowing you are doing right. You don't need anyone else's praise. Someday your husband's success will be your success.

3. Being a wife and mother is the highest calling for me because I enjoy my children. The Bible says in Psalm 127:3, *"Lo, children are an heritage of the LORD: and the fruit of the womb is his reward."* Children are a gift from the Lord. How special is that? Just like many things in life, rearing children is not always easy and fun. There are hard times and trying of your patience times, but children are a gift from the Lord. We have been given a calling, and that is to help our husband rear our children in the nurture and admonition of the Lord. That is a pretty high calling if you ask me. It calls for a mom to be a servant 24/7. It includes a lot of training, patience, and love. But with God's help, it can be a rewarding calling.

We are preparing the next generation of moms and dads. I want to be sure that they are good ones. In Ezekiel 16:44 the Bible says, *"Behold, every one that useth proverbs shall use this proverb against thee, saying, As is the mother, so is her daughter."* Wow! That is scary to me sometimes! I want to train my daughters to be better than me—without my weaknesses. To do that, I better make sure I am training them in the nurture and admonition of the Lord.

I show my kids that I enjoy being a mom by how I act during my day. By the way, this means I prepare meals and clean house. You can be preparing for these days now by treating your brothers and sisters the right way, by teaching a Sunday school class, or by working in a nursery. Work on having patience, doing what is right to do, and not doing what you want to do. Definitely take time to appreciate what your mom does for you now.

4. Being a wife and mother is the highest calling to me because I choose to make it a high calling. The Bible says Acts 11:23, *"Who, when he came, and had seen the grace of God, was glad, and exhorted them all, that with **purpose of heart** they would cleave unto the Lord."* The Lord created me and most of you to be a helpmeet and then a mother. Psalm 113:9 says, *"He maketh the barren woman to keep house, and to be a joyful mother of children. Praise ye the LORD."* The Lord not only made us to be a help meet, a keeper of the home, and the mother of children, but a joyful wife and mother at that!

That is where Acts 11:23 comes in. We as women need to purpose in our heart that we are going to do what we are made to do and do it the way God intended for it to be done. We will find that we are truly happy and joyful when we do things God's way. What a blessed life He has for us. He knew we would be the happiest when we are serving our husband, our children, or those whom He has for us to serve.

Being a wife and mother is the most wonderful job in the world. Let's choose to make being a wife and mother our highest calling. The Lord thinks it is. If a husband and children are in your future, then know that the Lord does not make mistakes, He must trust you an awful lot and have confidence that you are becoming the best wife and mother for your husband and children that you could possibly become.

I do not assume to know God's will for other women. I can only speak of God's leading in my life. I will never know if I could have made it as a business woman in today's society, but I do know I do **not** consider myself a poor, unfortunate soul. To the contrary, I feel very rich to have a man I respect and admire who loves and cherishes me; and I am also very fortunate to have five children I love more than life itself who call me Mom.

Instructions
for Challenge Pages

When you have completed the assignments for all ten challenge pages, copy or remove the pages from your booklet and send them to Christian Womanhood, 8400 Burr Street, Crown Point, Indiana 46307. You will receive a gift from Christian Womanhood for completing these challenges. We look forward to hearing from you.

– Jaclynn Weber

CHAPTER ONE

God's Plan for Your Life
Challenge Page

1.   Write your parents a thank-you note and thank them specifically for something they have done for you.

> ☐ Date Completed_____

2.   Write your pastor and pastor's wife a note of appreciation.

> ☐ Date Completed_____

3.   Memorize Luke 12:48b, "*For unto whomsoever much is given, of him shall be much required: and to whom men have committed much, of him they will ask the more.*" Write this verse on a card and post it where you will see it daily.

> ☐ Date Completed_____

Write the verse in the space provided below.

_____

_____

_____

_____

_____

CHAPTER TWO

How to Have a Good Spirit
Challenge Page

1. Do something anonymously for someone in your school. In the space provided, record what you did and for whom.

_____

_____

_____

2. Make a prayer list or add five things to your prayer list.

3. Make a "praise" list of at least ten things to praise God for and go through this list each day for a week.

4. Tell a friend about something good that God has done for you. In the space provided, record what you said.

_____

_____

_____

CHAPTER THREE

How to Deal With Rejection

Challenge Page

1.   Write a note to someone in your youth group who is struggling and tell the person something you like about her. Record the name of the person to whom you gave your letter.

☐ Name_____

2.   Stay after school and help a teacher with a project. In the space provided, record the name of the teacher and what you did to help.

_____

_____

_____

3.   Give ten sincere compliments a day for five days and check off each compliment for each day.

Days	Check one box for each compliment given.									
Day One										
Day Two										
Day Three										
Day Four										
Day Five										

4.   Memorize five verses that talk about God's love for us and record the references.

1.	4.
2.	5.
3.	

5. Look up 15 verses on forgiveness. Record the references and sum up what you learned from each verse.

1.	
2.	
3.	
4.	
5.	
6.	
7.	
8.	
9.	
10.	
11.	
12.	
13.	
14.	
15.	

The Beauty of Boldness
Challenge Page

1. Look up the definition of *boldness* and write it in the space provided.

_____

_____

_____

2. Write down an area of your life where you need more boldness and ask God each day for boldness in that area. The area in which I need more boldness is _____

_____

_____

3. Pass out 50 tracts.

> ☐ Date Completed_____

4. Win someone to the Lord in your neighborhood or a friend's neighborhood. Record the name of the person.

> ☐ Name_____

5. Look up and write the six parts to the armor of God (Ephesians 6) that will shield you from Satan's darts and give you boldness:

6. Walk the aisle at your church on a Sunday and pray for God to give you boldness.

> ☐ Date Completed_____

CHAPTER FIVE

Have a Cabinet of Counselors
Challenge Page

1. Do a Bible study on the word *trust*. Look up ten verses and write down what you think they mean. Record the references and your thoughts.

1.	
2.	
3.	
4.	
5.	
6.	
7.	
8.	
9.	
10.	

2. Write a letter to your future husband in which you promise to stay pure until your wedding day.

> ☐ Date Completed_____

3. Make a list of your "cabinet" of counselors. Keep a copy for yourself and write the names in the spaces provided.

4. Make an appointment with one of your counselors whom you trust and ask him/her for some advice. Record the name of the counselor with whom you sought advice.

> ☐ Date Completed_____

CHAPTER SIX

Preparing for the Real World
Challenge Page

1. Check off each day for a week that you get up at the same time and read your Bible. Record the time and the Bible passage.

Days		Time	Bible Reading Passage
Monday	☐		
Tuesday	☐		
Wednesday	☐		
Thursday	☐		
Friday	☐		
Saturday	☐		
Sunday	☐		

2. Prepare dinner for the whole family and record your menu.

Menu	

3. Ask your mom to let you do the grocery shopping for a week. Make a list, get a set amount of money (from Dad or Mom), and record how much you spent.

$ given	$ spent
Items needed:	

4. Exercise for a week and write down what you did and how long you exercised.

Days	Time Spent	Type of Exercise
Monday		
Tuesday		
Wednesday		
Thursday		
Friday		
Saturday		
Sunday		

5. Make a list of all of the things for which you have to be thankful, then go through the list and thank God for each one.

CHAPTER SEVEN

Living by Faith
Challenge Page

1. Do a Bible study on faith. Look up 20 verses on faith. Give the reference of a verse that had special meaning to you. Why is this verse special to you?

1.	
2.	
3.	
4.	
5.	
6.	
7.	
8.	
9.	
10.	

11.	
12.	
13.	
14.	
15.	
16.	
17.	
18.	
19.	
20.	

2. Give an example of a time in your own life where you stepped out in faith, trusting only God to see you through. What did you learn from that experience?

_____

_____

3. Share the Gospel with a friend or loved one so that he may see your faith in action. Who was this person? What plans do you have to

disciple him to also live a life of faith? (i.e.; invite this person to church, encourage him in his daily walk with God, etc.) If you cannot think of a friend or loved one to witness to, begin a relationship with someone for the sole purpose of one day sharing your faith. Who is this person?

❒ Name_____

4. Set aside two different times during the day where you ask the Lord to strengthen your faith in Him. Here is an example of a prayer that will only take a few seconds. *"Lord, help me to live today how You want me to live, to do what You would have me to do. Help me to have faith in Your will and Your way and to trust You with my whole heart. I love You, Lord."* What times will you set aside?

Day	Time Spent	Time Spent

5. Write a thank you note to someone who has inspired you by their words or actions to live a life of faith. Record the name of that person in the space provided.

❒ Name_____

CHAPTER EIGHT

Building a Good Relationship With Your Siblings
Challenge Page

1. Write your sister or brother a note telling her/him what you like about her/him.

☐ Date completed_____

2. Buy a gift for a brother/sister and leave it somewhere where your sibling will find it. Record the gift you chose.

☐ Date completed_____
Gift purchased _____

3. Take a sibling or parent out to eat or shopping and pay for the outing. Record who you took and what you did.

☐ Outing _____
Name _____

4. If you have not already done so, add your siblings to your daily prayer list.

☐ Date Completed_____

CHAPTER NINE

No Regrets With My Mom
Challenge Page

1. What have you done for your mom lately? Plan something special to do for your mom.

☐ Date completed_____

2. Have you prayed for your mom? Pray for your mom today. Add her to your daily prayer list.

☐ Date completed_____

3. Give your mom a card, a gift, or another sweet reminder of your love. Write down what you did.

_____

_____

_____

_____

_____

4. Ask your mom's advice about something you are facing in your life right now.

_____

_____

_____

5. If you don't have a mother with whom you live, please find someone else like your pastor's wife or youth pastor's wife from whom you can seek advice. Who will be the person from whom you will seek advice?

☐ Name _____

CHAPTER TEN

The Highest Calling
Challenge Page

1. Ask your mom for some advice, and then do what she tells you. Check the space provided when you have followed her advice.

☐ Date completed_____

2. Ask your mom to teach your how to do something such as cook a meal, sew a garment, clean a room, etc. Record what you learned from your mother.

What I Have Learned From My Mom

3. Watch or go to a sporting event with your dad or brother. Record what you did together.

☐ Date completed_____

4. At dinner one evening, go around the table and tell something you love about each member of your family.

☐ Date completed_____

5. Clean the house for your mom and give her the day off.

☐ Date completed_____